JAM HANDS!

a DyslexiAssist Reader, Reading Level 1-2

No part of this publication may be reproduced, either in part or in whole, or stored in an electronic or retrieval system, or transmitted in any form or by any means, including electronic, mechanical, photocopying, recording, or otherwise, without the express written permission of the publisher. For information regarding permission, contact knowonder via email: editor@knowonder.com

All stories copyright Knowonder, LLC 2016. All rights reserved.
Published by Knowonder, LLC.

Stock photography and artwork from stock.adobe.com.
See http://knowonder.com/jam-hands-stock-photo for details.

ISBN: 978-15354393-1-2

A collection

of read aloud stories

perfect for 1st and 2nd

grade reading levels.

About DyslexiAssist™

Part of our mission at Knowonder! Publishing is to make literacy more effective. In order to fulfill that mission for children suffering from dyslexia we are proud to announce our new DyslexiAssist™ initiative: to publish each of our books in a special font designed to make reading easier for dyslexics. You can learn more about it on our website at:

www.knowonder.com/dyslexiassist

When reading with this new font, independent research shows that 84% of dyslexics read faster, 77% read with fewer mistakes, and 76% recommend the font to others who suffer from dyslexia.

But the magic isn't just in the font. We take extra care to make the font an appropriate size, give proper spacing to letters in the words, make sure that there are the exact right number of words on each line, and so much more! The layout of the book is just as important. We go to extra lengths to make sure all the stars are aligned so they, too, can know the wonder of reading.

Reading stories is not only fun, but also critical for learning. We hope this new initiative can now bring the same love and joy of reading and learning to your home!

Table of Contents

- 4   About DyslexiAssist
- 9   Jam Hands! (6 pg.)
- 15   Go to Sleep, Bunny (11 pg.)
- 26   The Cheesy Man in the Moon (6 pg.)
- 32   The Snooze Shoes (8 pg.)
- 40   Buddy (7 pg.)
- 47   My Hair GREW (5 pg.)
- 52   The Friday Night Fairy (8 pg.)
- 60   The Honey Bear (5 pg.)
- 65   The Best Horse in the World (4 pg.)
- 69   Magic Wrinkles (6 pg.)
- 75   Monster Rapids (9 pg.)
- 84   Cookie Time (7 pg.)
- 91   The Brave Seagull (6 pg.)
- 97   The Mysterious K.W.L.B. (9 pg.)

Dedicated to my young friends
who struggle with dyslexia.
Remember this –
if you let them,
life's challenges will
make you **stronger**.

JAM HANDS!

by Rolli

I've got JAM HANDS! From eating peanut butter and jam sandwiches! That's my favorite sandwich!

Lucky for me, jam hands come in handy.

One time I was eating peanut butter and jam sandwiches and I heard a lady scream, "Help! HELP!"

I looked out the window. A building was on fire. I ran outside with my jam hands. I climbed up the building with my sticky hands. They worked just like suction cups. I climbed up to — I think it was the 99th floor. A lady was waving a hanky out the window.

"Help! HELP!" she screamed again.

"I'll help you," I said.

The lady stared at me.

"How?" she said.

"I've got jam hands," I said.

"Oh, okay," she said. Then she hopped onto my back. And I carried her back down.

Another time I was eating peanut butter and jam sandwiches and the phone rang. It's hard answering the phone with jam hands. It took me a while.

"Hello?" I said.

"HI!" said a loud voice. "IS THIS THE KID WITH THE JAM HANDS?"

"Yup," I said.

"MEET ME IN THE MAYOR'S OFFICE RIGHT AWAY!"

"Sure thing," I said. "Hey wait — who is this?"

"THIS IS THE MAYOR!"

"Oh, okay," I said. And I hung up.

When I got to the mayor's office, he was pacing back and forth.

"I'LL BE HONEST WITH YOU, KID — THIS IS A BIG-TIME PROBLEM. MAJOR! MEGA! I'M NOT SURE YOU CAN HANDLE IT."

"I'm listening," I said.

"SEE THIS VENT IN THE FLOOR? MY PEN FELL DOWN THERE. IT WAS MY FAVORITE PEN. IF I STICK MY FINGERS DOWN THE VENT HOLES, I CAN TOUCH THE PEN, BUT I CAN'T QUITE GET IT. CAN YOU HELP ME, KID? CAN YOU?"

"I'll try," I said.

I knelt down and poked my finger down the vent holes. When I touched the pen, it stuck to my fingers.

I pulled it out.

"Here you go," I said.

"THANKS, KID! YOU'RE THE BEST! BETTER THAN THE BEST! YOU'RE AWESOME! ONE DAY, I'LL NAME A STREET AFTER YOU. HOW DOES JAM KID AVENUE SOUND?"

"Sounds just fine," I said.

This one other time — oh, it was yesterday — I didn't want to go to bed, so just before the sun went down I touched it with my finger, and it stopped moving. It just stuck to the jam. I am not lying. Even ask my Mom.

But having jam hands isn't **ALL** great. It's easier to catch a ball, but way harder to throw one. I can't really fluff my pillow. And when I wash my hands, I'm just a regular kid again. That stinks.

But all I have to do is eat another peanut butter and jam sandwich...

And I've got **JAM HANDS** again!

the end.

Go to Sleep, Bunny!

by Kathleen Murphy

"Goodnight, Robbie," said Robbie's mom as she kissed him goodnight.

"Just one more story, Mommy?" asked Robbie.

"No more stories, Rob. Two stories and then goodnight, that was our deal," said Mommy. "Sweet dreams," she called and left the room.

Robbie cuddled underneath his favorite blanket. He rubbed the soft, satiny edge across his cheek. He rolled over to face the shelf where his stuffed animals sat.

"Goodnight, everybody," said Rob.

"Goodnight, Rob," said Snake. Hiss, hiss hiss.

"Goodnight, Rob," said Pig. Grunt, grunt, grunt.

"Goodnight, Rob," said Mouse. Squeak, squeak, squeak.

"Goodnight, Rob," said Bunny. Twitch, twitch, twitch.

All was quiet in his room. The only sound Rob could hear was the sound of his mother working on the computer... tap, tap, tap, tap. He closed his eyes and tried to sleep.

Just then a voice called out, "I can't sleep."

Robbie opened his eyes and looked at his animals.

"Who said that?" he asked.

"Not me," said Snake. Hiss, hiss, hiss.

"Not me," said Pig. Grunt, grunt, grunt.

"Not me," said Mouse. Squeak, squeak, squeak.

"It's me," whispered Bunny.

"What's the matter?" asked Robbie.

"I can't sleep," answered Bunny. "I'm not tired."

Robbie jumped out of bed. "I'll tell Mommy." He rushed to the door and called out, "Mommy! Bunny can't sleep! He's not tired."

"You'll be tired tomorrow if you don't get some sleep, Robbie," answered Mommy.

"But it's not me. It's Bunny," explained Robbie.

"Well then, tell Bunny. Goodnight Robbie!"

"Goodnight, Mommy." Robbie dove back into bed.

"Did you hear that, Bunny?"

"Yes, Rob," he answered.

"Just try and go to sleep, okay?"

"Okay," said Bunny.

All was quiet in the room again. Robbie closed his eyes. One minute passed until...

"I can't sleep."

Robbie opened his eyes. "What is it now, Bunny?" he asked.

"I can't sleep when I'm thirsty," said Bunny.

"I'll get you some water," said Robbie as he climbed out of bed. He opened the door and called out, "Mommy! Bunny can't sleep. He's thirsty!"

"Oh, Rob," sighed Mommy. "Didn't you have a drink before bed?"

"But it's not for me," Rob explained. "It's for Bunny." He listened for his mother's answer, but she didn't give one. Then he heard shhhh, drip, drip, drip. His mother appeared in his doorway with a cup of water in her hand.

"Drink up and then get back to bed," said Mommy. "No more fooling."

"But Mommy, I told you. It's not me," pleaded Rob. "It's Bunny!"

"Then tell Bunny if he doesn't get some sleep, he'll be a cranky rabbit tomorrow!" She blew a kiss to Rob and left the room.

Robbie carried the water over to Bunny. "Drink this and then go to sleep." Bunny took the cup. Sluuurp, glug, glug, glug. He gulped the water and handed the empty cup back to Rob. "Thank you, Rob."

"You're welcome, Bunny."

Once again, all was quiet in the room. Robbie yawned and stretched. He closed his eyes and tried to fall asleep.

"Robbie," whispered Bunny.

"What is it now?" asked Rob.

"I'm scared of monsters," said Bunny.

"Silly Bunny!" said Snake. Hiss, hiss, hiss.

"What monsters?" asked Pig. Grunt, grunt, grunt.

"I'm not scared," said Mouse. Squeak, squeak, squeak.

Rob sat up in his bed. "There's no monster in here, Bunny," he said.

"Could you check and make sure?" asked Bunny.

"I'll get Mommy," said Rob. He jumped out of bed and ran to his mother's room.

"What are you doing out of bed?" she asked.

"Could you check for monsters, Mommy?" asked Rob.

"Robbie, you know there's no such thing as monsters," she said.

"I know," said Rob. "It's Bunny. He wants us to check for him."

"Will it help him get to sleep?" Mom asked.

"Yep," said Rob. "Let's go." He grabbed his mother's hand and they walked back into Rob's bedroom. Robbie followed his mother around the room as she searched.

She looked inside the closet. "I don't see any monsters in here," she said. Next she peeked behind the door. "No monsters here either." Finally she knelt down and looked underneath Rob's bed. "Any monsters hiding here?" she called out. "No monsters, Rob. Now back to bed." She tucked Robbie in and kissed his forehead.

"I'll tell Bunny," said Rob.

"Goodnight for the last time," said Mom as she

left the room.

"No monsters, Bunny," said Rob.

"Thank you, Rob," said Bunny.

"You're welcome. Now go to sleep!"

The room was quiet, except for the sound of yawns and murmurs. Two minutes passed and then…

"I can't sleep."

"Not again!" said Snake. Hiss, hiss, hiss.

"Oh, brother!" said Pig. Grunt, grunt, grunt.

"My goodness!" said Mouse. Squeak, squeak, squeak.

Sniff, sniff, sniff…"WAAAAAAAA!" cried Bunny.

"Don't cry, Bunny," said Rob. "Why can't you sleep this time?" he asked.

Bunny tried to speak through the tears. "I'm... I...I ... I'm lonely," he blurted out.

Rob smiled. "Would you like to come and sleep over here?" he asked.

"Oh, yes," said Bunny happily. He hopped off the shelf and onto Rob's bed. He curled up next to Rob and closed his eyes.

"All better?" asked Rob.

"Yes, Rob," said Bunny. "Thank you."

"Excuse me, Rob," said Snake. "I'm lonely, too."

"So am I," said Pig.

"Me too," said Mouse.

Rob giggled. "Okay. Everybody come on over."

Snake coiled up in a ball beside Rob. Pig rolled

over and flopped down by Rob's feet. Mouse scampered up to Rob's pillow, where he lay down in the softness.

Again all was quiet in the room. "Goodnight, everybody," said Rob.

"Goodnight, Rob," said Snake. Hiss, hiss, hiss.

"Goodnight, Rob," said Pig. Grunt, grunt, grunt.

"Goodnight, Rob," said Mouse. Squeak, squeak, squeak.

But Bunny didn't answer. He had fallen fast asleep. Snore, snore, snore.

the end.

The Cheesy Man in the Moon

by Susan York Meyers

Walter stared out the window and gazed up at his friend, that cheesy Man in the Moon. Walter waved. But no wink, no blink in return. Just a sad frown, a smile turned upside down.

Something was wrong with his friend, the cheesy Man in the Moon.

If his friend needed help, then Walter must go. So he grabbed a spoon from a kitchen drawer. One never knew when one would need a spoon. He slipped out the back door and ran through the tall, green grass.

He had to get up high, as high as he could climb. Walter sprinted past the oak tree. He scurried past the playground, its swings silent in the moonlight. The goldfish in the pond darted to and fro as he hurried by.

At the top of the hill, Walter stood among the low floating clouds. Their softness tickled, but he had no time to giggle. However, he did use his spoon to grab a nibble. The scoop of cloud tasted like the marshmallows his mom put in his cocoa.

No time to waste—Walter had to help his friend. He stood on his tiptoes then reached out and grabbed the edge of the cloud. He scrambled onto its fluffy lightness. Walter floated through the sky amid the twinkling stars.

But Walter soon realized the cloud drifted far too low to reach the moon. He spied a patch of star dust. Using his spoon like a paddle, he sailed toward the dusty trail.

Not too fast, Walter thought. I've got to time it just right.

Now! He leaped from the cloud onto the sparkly trail. Walter skipped across the star dust, close—but not yet to his goal.

The Man in the Moon saw Walter's problem and sent a moonbeam. Walter reached high.

Oh, no, he missed!

Walter got down low and jumped real high.

Another miss!

How can I be taller? Walter thought. Ah ha! I can use my spoon. He hooked the moonbeam and rode it to the moon.

"What's wrong, my friend?" Walter asked as he landed.

Big tears squeezed from the Man in the Moon's

eyes. "It hurts," he said. "Right there."

A shooting star was lodged in his front tooth! "I'll get you out of this spot," Walter said.

He wiggled the star. He jiggled the star. But it was stuck

   tight.

Was all lost?

No! Walter pulled out his spoon and got to digging. He took the utmost care not to hurt his friend. The soft cheese crumbled away. "Just a little more," Walter said.

Pop! The star burst free!

"Thank you," she squealed as she danced point to point.

"Thank you, Walter," said the Man in the Moon. "You've proven a loyal friend this day."

"Hop on," the shooting star said. "I'll take you home to your bed."

Walter climbed to her tip-top point. "Goodbye!" he shouted to his friend.

The star and Walter raced through the night sky. She shot him straight into his bed.

Just before Walter closed his eyes, he looked up and waved.

And in return, his friend, the cheesy Man in the Moon, gave Walter a slow wink and a smile.

the end.

The Snooze Shoes

by Rolli

Well, the Snooze Shoes fell out of the sky one day and landed — plop — right in my hands. I knew they were Snooze Shoes 'cuz there was a tag on them that said "Snooze Shoes." So I ripped it off. You're supposed to.

"Hmm..." I said. "If these really are Snooze

Shoes, then whoever wears them should fall asleep instantly."

I decided to test them out.

Mom was upstairs, dusting vases.

"Dum-de-dum, dum-de-dum, tidy-tidy," she was humming to herself. (Why are moms like this?)

So I said, "Hey, Mom! Try on these shoes!"

"Ooh, I love trying on shoes!" she said.

She slipped them on...

Curled up on the floor...

And started to snore.

"Honk-a-chooo, honk-a-chooo." (Everyone in my family snores like this.)

"Awesome!" I said. 'Cuz now I could do whatever

I wanted.

Like jump on the couch.

And ride the dog.

And eat marshmallows — lots of 'em.

Yup, I could do whatever I wanted. That is, until Dad got home.

"I'm hoooooome!" he sang, slamming the door shut behind him.

So I ran back upstairs, tiptoed up to mom, and carefully pulled the Snooze Shoes off her feet.

I must've been gentle, 'cuz she kept right on snoring.

Then I flew back downstairs.

"Daddy!" I said, skipping up to him.

"What did you do?" he asked, lifting his eyebrows.

"Nothing!" I said (even if it was kind of a lie).

"Wanna try on some shoes?"

"Ug! I hate shoes!" he said. It was true. The first thing he always did when he got home was kick them off and wiggle his bare toes.

"Pleeeease?" I said as sweetly as possible.

"Well, all right," he said.

So he slipped them on....

Flopped back into the armchair....

And started to snore.

"Honk-a-chooo, honk-a-chooo."

"Double awesome!" I cried. 'Cuz it was. I could do anything — times two!

So I dressed up the cat.

And rolled oranges down the stairs.

And ate triple fudge brownies (lots of 'em).

I was invincible. That is, until my big brother got home. He came in the kitchen door.

"Hey, where is everybody?" he asked.

So I raced into the living room, tiptoed up to Dad, and carefully pulled the Snooze Shoes off his feet.

I must've been really gentle 'cuz he kept on snoring.

I ran back into the kitchen.

"What are you lookin' at?" said my big brother, scrunching up his eyebrows.

"Nothin,'" I said. "Wanna try on some shoes?"

"NO! I DON'T WANNA TRY ON ANY STUPID SHOES!" he cried. Big brothers can be like that.

"Pleeease," I said as sweetly as possible.

"NO WAY!"

That kind of thing doesn't usually work on big brothers.

So we wrestled...

And fought...

And got all tangled up, like a kite in your neighbor's hair.

But in the end, the Snooze Shoes were on his feet, and he was fast asleep.

"Honk-a-chooo, honk-a-chooo."

"Victory!" I cried. I mean, he was older than me. I

could do anything — times three!

To celebrate, I jumped over the couch.

And let the hamster out.

And ate fruit snacks (lots of 'em).

It was pretty amazing.

And then...it wasn't.

'Cuz once you've jumped around, played, and eaten all the snacks you can find, there really isn't much left to do.

It was pretty lonely. I mean, it was bedtime, and there was no one to tuck me in.

So I went to the kitchen.

And lifted the Snooze Shoes off my brother's smelly feet. He didn't even wake up.

Then I skipped upstairs, climbed into bed, fluffed my pillow, and screamed once, as loud as possible.

"EEEEEEEEEEEEEEEEEE!"

I heard three big yawns. Then three big people shuffled into the room.

"What happened?" they all said, rubbing their eyes.

"Nothing," I said, smiling.

Which was kind of a lie.

Oh, well.

the end.

Buddy

by Mary McClellan

Natalie walked into her bedroom and found Buddy surrounded by chewed up papers. "Oh, no. Buddy, you've been a bad dog," she said.

Buddy hid under the bed and watched as she

picked up what was left of her homework folder and her new dictionary.

"I'm going to be in trouble for leaving my things on the floor where you could get them. Did the cover of the dictionary taste bad? It's the only part you didn't eat."

Buddy inched farther back under the bed.

"How can I do my homework without my folder?" she asked. "I have to study for a test."

"I'm sorry," a voice said.

Natalie stopped and looked around. "Who said that?"

Buddy looked around, too.

Natalie got down on her hands and knees and

looked under the bed. "Is someone under there with you, Buddy?"

"No."

"Buddy, is that you talking?" she asked.

"I...I guess it is. Yes," said Buddy, with a look of surprise on his face.

Natalie stared at him. "Come out here."

Buddy crawled out from under the bed and sat in front of her.

"When did you start talking?" she asked.

"This is the first time." He scratched his ear with his hind leg. "I'm just as surprised as you are."

"How did this happen?" Natalie asked.

"I don't know, but I might be able to figure it out

if I had a biscuit."

"You always want a biscuit. Is that all you think about?" she asked.

"Yes, most of the time."

"You're thinking about food, and I'm worrying about tomorrow's spelling test. I need to study those words that sound alike but have different meanings."

"Like t-h-e-r-e and t-h-e-i-r?" asked Buddy.

Natalie stared at Buddy, her mouth open. "How do you know that?"

Buddy rolled on his back. "I don't know. I didn't know it when I woke up this morning."

"Wait a minute," Natalie said. "What's two plus four?"

"Six," said Buddy.

"Can you name a planet?" she asked.

"Earth."

"Buddy, I know what happened," said Natalie.

He sat up. "What?"

"You learned everything you ate!" she said.

"I did?"

"Yes. Since you ate my dictionary, you can talk. And you know about spelling, math, and space because you ate my homework folder."

"You're right. I didn't know any of this before I chewed up your things."

"This is incredible," she said.

"Does this mean I can have a biscuit?"

"Buddy, you can have two biscuits."

"Wow. Who knew talking could be this much fun? I wish you'd left your papers on the floor before!"

Natalie laughed.

"Could you tell your teacher your dog ate your homework so you couldn't study for the test?"

"Teachers hear that all the time."

Buddy was surprised. "You mean dogs everywhere chew homework?"

"No, but kids say that when they haven't studied."

"But it's true," said Buddy.

"We know that. I'll have to think of...wait, I've got it."

"What?"

"You're going to help me pass the test," said Natalie.

"How?"

"You know the material, so you can help me study."

"That's a great idea," said Buddy. "Let's get the biscuits and get started."

the end.

My Hair GREW

by Rolli

My hair grew too much so my mom took me to see Sheila. I like Sheila because she has a green necklace, and she's careful with my ears. If I look sad she says, "Tell me all about it." Then I do tell her, and I feel a lot better.

Sheila cut my hair pretty short that day. My mom kept saying, "Shorter, Sheila, shorter." So she just kept cutting it. I wasn't too sure about this haircut, but I didn't say that.

When we got home I looked in the mirror and cried. I yelled, "MY HAIR IS TOO LITTLE FOR ME!" Because it was.

My mom said it looked cute, and she was sure if I slept on it I'd like it in the morning.

I slept on my hair all night, and when I woke up I looked in the mirror. Nope. I still didn't like it. My hair was definitely too short. I hated it. So I decided to grow my hair. You can if you really try.

I grew it one inch, then another inch, then one more inch. It still looked kind of short, though. So I grew it one foot, then another foot, then one more foot. I still wasn't sure. So I grew it one mile, then another mile, then one more mile. Then I meant to stop, but I accidentally grew it **TWENTY-FIVE THOUSAND MILES**. It's hard to control your hair sometimes.

My hair stretched all the way around the planet Earth. It was the planet Hair, now. When I looked at all that hair, I cried. I yelled, "**MY HAIR IS TOO BIG FOR ME!**" Because it was.

Then Sheila poked her head up out of the hair.

"Sit down," she said. So I did.

"How was your day?" she asked, taking out her scissors.

"Crummy," I said.

"Tell me all about it," she said as she started cutting.

She snipped off one mile, then another mile, then one more mile.

She snipped off TWENTY-FIVE THOUSAND MILES.

She snipped off one foot, then another foot, then one more foot.

She snipped off one inch, then another inch, then one last inch.

I looked in the mirror. My hair looked just right.

"Thanks, Sheila!" I said.

"No problem," she said.

Then she swept up all the hair.

I love getting haircuts.

the end.

The Friday Night Fairy

by Jill Tinker

The storm was raging outside. Huge raindrops bounced off the roof and flashes of lightning lit up the dark sky. Georgie hid under the pillows. She wanted her Mum... or even her Dad. She had Donna. There was a loud bang. The thunder rolled on and on. Georgie tried to shout out. No sound came.

Donna was downstairs. It was twelve steps away. That was all. Georgie had counted them on her way to bed. She liked numbers. They made her feel better. Counting made her forget what was worrying her. And lots of songs had numbers in them.

Every night her Mum sang 'There were ten in the bed'. Georgie always fell asleep before the end.

Friday nights were different. Donna looked after her. She lived two doors up and she couldn't sing. She couldn't catch a ball. She couldn't skip. She couldn't do jigsaws.

There was one thing she was good at. She told

great stories. Georgie didn't know if they were real. They were funny and they always had happy endings. She wanted to believe them. But Donna told lies!

"We had such a good time last week." She told Georgie's Mum.

That was a lie.

"Georgie knows lots of games."

That was true. She knew tons of games. She never got to play them though. Donna sent her to bed.

"You need loads of sleep at your age." She said.

Was that a lie? Georgie didn't know.

At Christmas her Mum said

"Santa only comes to girls who are asleep."

When she lost her first tooth she said

"The tooth fairy waits for you to go to sleep before she swaps the tooth for money."

Why didn't they want to see her awake? She wondered.

Maybe the tooth fairy had worse spots than Donna. She must have worse teeth. She took children's spares. She must have a huge mouth to need so many. It must have enormous gaps waiting to be filled.

Georgie shivered. She was scared. Too scared to be alone.

"Donna!"

Georgie tiptoed to the top of the stairs. She looked down. She started to walk down.

She started to count down. Three...two...one.

"What are you doing? You should be in bed." Donna didn't look pleased to see her.

"I can't sleep."

"It's only thunder." Donna grinned. "You're not scared, are you?"

"No." Georgie lied. "Are you?"

"Course not."

There was another bang.

Georgie jumped.

Donna jumped too. Her face was red. She looked

scared.

Georgie didn't want to be alone.

"Have you ever seen the tooth fairy?" She asked. If she could just keep Donna talking she needn't be on her own.

"No." Donna didn't sound as though she wanted to talk.

"Or Santa?"

"No. They're not real, you know."

"They are. I got a pound for my last tooth and I always get presents at Christmas."

"So what does this tooth fairy look like then?"

"Ask her." Georgie pointed to the window.

A flash of lightning lit up a pretty face. Her dress sparkled. She smiled and waved her wand.

Georgie waved back.

Donna ran up the stairs.

The door opened. Her fairy Mum and Santa Dad were back from the party.

"What's the matter with Donna?" Her Mum asked.

"Anyone would think she'd never seen a fairy." Her Dad pulled off the Santa beard.

"She hasn't."

Georgie's Mum and Dad laughed.

"Maybe we should have warned her we'd be coming back in fancy dress. It's not as though we're monsters though." Dad said.

"Come on, Georgie." Her Mum took her hand.

"How many in the bed?"

"Ten."

They went up the stairs singing "There were ten in the bed".

And found Donna hiding under the bed.

the end.

The Honey Bear

by Rolli

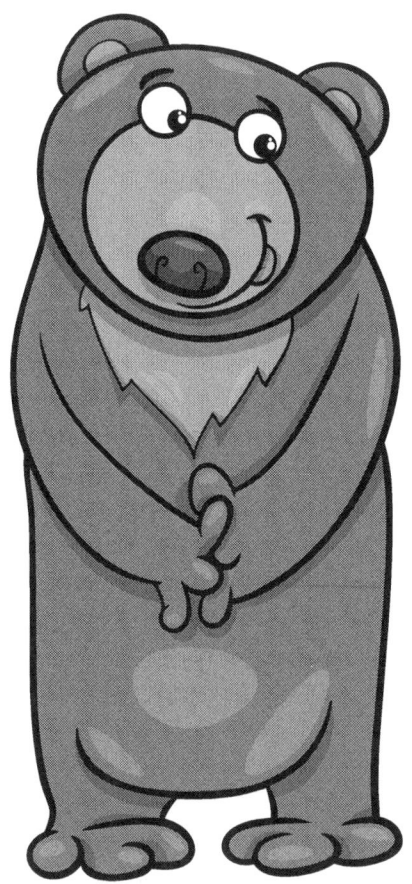

I like most bears. But NOT the one that gives me licks!

When I go outside, he jumps up and gives me licks. My hair sticks straight up. I HATE that.

He's a tall, brown bear. He has gold spots. He's sort of fat.

Now, I have to look out the window to see if he's there. If he is, I just work on my drawings or my submarine. If he isn't, I open the door. I take one step. I take one more step. If it looks safe, I start walking. I'll either have a normal day or that bear will jump out from behind a bush or a tree and lick me all over.

"Ugh!" I'll say, when he does this. "You, sicko! Gross!" And I'll run back inside.

Once he was laying down flat like the living room

carpet, and when I stepped on him, he bounced up and gave me licks.

"Ugh!" I said. "That's disgusting, you know?" And I ran back inside and had a bath.

Last week I forgot to check, and I just ran outside. I was working hard on my drawings, and I wasn't thinking! The bear was standing on the front porch. I ran straight into his arms! He gave me a bear hug and licked my face till it was soaking wet.

That was it. I decided I was **FED UP**.

"Ugh!" I said. "How would you like it if I did that to you? Hey? Would you like it if I gave **YOU** licks, bear? Huh?"

The bear just stared at me. I don't think he

understood. Bears don't always understand. I needed to show him. So....

I gave him a lick.

The bear looked surprised.

I gave him another lick.

The bear looked shocked.

"Mmm," I said. "Delicious!"

It was true. He really was delicious, this bear. He tasted exactly like honey, like you put on bread. Maybe he was a Honey Bear. I decided he was.

I licked the Honey Bear again. And again. I gave that bear so many licks, his furs all stuck out like on a cat! It looked hilarious. I think he felt embarrassed. Cuz he ran off.

I still see that Honey Bear sometimes. Only he doesn't give me licks now. Sometimes we even play, if there's no other bears around. We play tag, because I'm faster. Maybe we'll even be friends one day.

Maybe.

I've gotta go work on my submarine.

the end.

The Best Horse in the World

by Shari L. Klase

One day, Daddy asked Tommy, "Do you want a horse?"

"Oh yes, Daddy! Please!" Tommy said.

So Daddy spent all the next day in his workshop in the basement. He worked and worked. When he was done, he gave Tommy the horse he had made.

The horse was black all over. It had a thick stick body and a carved wooden head. It had a mouth and nostrils and ears. It had big, brown eyes, all carefully painted by Daddy.

"Thank you, Daddy!" Tommy said. "He's pretty! I'm going to call him Tonka!"

Every day, Tommy rode Tonka to wonderful adventures in his back yard. Tommy was a knight in shining armor. He was an Indian on the plains. He was a cowboy on the range. He was a jockey at the races.

Tonka was the best horse in the world. He ate the greenest grass. He drank the freshest water. He slept on the sweetest straw.

When it was time for bed, Tommy put Tonka away

in his toy chest in the basement.

Tonka waited patiently for tomorrow's adventures.

But the day came when Tommy was too old to ride Tonka. It made him sad to leave Tonka in the toy chest and he promised he would never forget him.

Tommy grew up. He went to school and got a job. He married the woman he loved and had a child of his own. And he kept his promise to Tonka.

Tommy asked his daughter, Crissy, "Do you want a horse?"

"Oh yes, Daddy! Please!" Crissy said.

So Tommy took Tonka out of the old toy chest in his parents' basement. He dusted Tonka off and painted him so that he looked brand new. Then he gave Tonka to Crissy.

"Thank you, Daddy," Crissy said. "He's pretty! What's his name?"

Tommy said, "I used to call him Tonka. You can give him any name you like."

Crissy said, "I'll call him Tonka, too."

Crissy rode Tonka to many wonderful adventures in her back yard. Crissy was a princess. She was an Indian on the plains. She was a cowgirl on the range. She was a jockey at the races.

And Tonka was the best horse in the world.

the end.

Magic Wrinkles

by Allyn M. Stotz

"Hey Brady, look at me," said my big brother Jesse. "Grrr... I'm the wrinkle monster! It's your turn in the bathtub now." He wiggled his ugly wrinkled fingers in my face as he passed by me in the hallway.

No way was I turning into a wrinkle monster. The kids at school would laugh at me. I ran to my bedroom.

A few minutes later, Mommy came into my room. "Why aren't you in the bathtub?"

"I'm sick, Mommy," I said, using my best hoarse voice.

She felt my head. "You don't feel hot."

Oops. "I could get sick again from the water though. Can I wait until later?"

Mommy crossed her arms. "I'm too tired to argue. Tonight, there will be no excuses, young man."

Whenever mommy called me young man, that usually meant she was mad. I knew I'd have to come up with a good plan for tonight. Maybe I could run away before supper? No — that wouldn't work. I'd miss Mommy's spaghetti and be too hungry. Maybe I could say I was sleepy. No — that wouldn't work. I'd have to go to bed early and miss my favorite show on Animal Planet. I know, I could pretend to cough and sneeze. No — that wouldn't work. Mommy would make me take yucky medicine.

I finally gave up and went downstairs.

That night, after supper, my stomach felt funny. I knew what was coming. Jesse whispered in my ear as he got up from the supper table, "It's almost time for that bath, little bro. Hope your fingers don't get all shriveled up, just like a wicked old hag of a witch, ahahahaha!"

What am I going to do? I don't want to get creepy wrinkles! I went to my room and plopped down at my desk. I felt confused about why my fingers never wrinkled before when I took a bath. Maybe I just didn't notice them?

I looked at my fingers and toes. "Nope, not wrinkly."

I thought to myself that maybe only old people got the wrinkles? Jesse was 15 years old but I didn't think that seemed old.

Could girls get wrinkles too? I wondered.

Maybe Jesse tricked me and the wrinkles on his fingers were fake? But they looked so real.

I decided to do a test. I ran to the bathroom sink, climbed on my step stool, and filled it with water. I got rubber ducky to play with so I wouldn't get bored. Before I knew it, I had played in the sink with my hands in the water for about a million hours. My fingers came out all wrinkly, just like a wicked old... ewww! I ran back to my room to wait.

I paced back and forth.

Then I heard Mommy yell, "Brady, five minutes to bath time!"

My eyes got big. Wrinkles be gone, wrinkles be gone. I took a deep breath before taking my hands out of my pocket and... no more wrinkles!

Just then, Jesse leaped in my room. "Is the fraidy-cat ready for me to start his bath water?"

I got my PJ's and smiled. "Yep, let's go."

After my bath, I ran downstairs and jumped on Mommy's lap.

"Oooh, you smell so fresh and clean," she said.

"I took my bath. Did you know that if you stay in the water a long time, your fingers and toes get all wrinkly? And you know what else?"

Mommy said, "What my good boy?"

"They go away, just like magic!"

the end.

Monster Rapids

by Jill Nogales

"Hey, this water is cold!" Grady yelped as he stepped barefoot into the river.

"Come on, Grady," I said. "Let's jump into the raft before we get any wetter."

"Are you sure about this, Kyle?" Grady asked. He shivered. "The river looks kind of rough. And it's moving pretty fast. Do you have any idea how deep it is?"

"Don't worry," I said. "All you need to know is that rafting trips are fun and exciting."

Grady is a tough guy. He really is. Except when it comes to water. Then he's a chicken. I can say that because we have been best friends since we were napping with teddy bears. It's not like he doesn't know how to swim. We took five years of swimming lessons together.

"Where's Tom?" Grady asked. "I thought he was coming rafting with us."

Tom is my big brother. He taught me everything I know about rafting. Basically, you need a raft, a river, and a life vest. Pretty simple, right?

"Hey Tom, over here!" I yelled.

Tom headed toward me and Grady. Dad was helping him carry his canoe.

"Wow, that's a cool canoe," Grady said as Tom and Dad launched the canoe into the water.

"Thanks," Tom said. "It's new. Are you ready, guys? Let's go for a ride!"

Grady and I jumped into our raft. Dad gave Tom's canoe a shove. Tom hopped into it as it glided into the river.

"I'll pick you up by the Wilson Bridge," Dad yelled as we floated away.

Tom's canoe came up beside our raft. He splashed water on us with his paddle. Tom seemed to think this was funny, until Grady and I splashed him back.

"You guys better stop messing around," Tom said. "Here comes the first set of rapids."

Grady checked the straps on his life vest. He gripped the side of the raft as we got bumped and tossed around by the rapids.

"Yahoo!" Tom yelled. He enjoys a wild ride.

When we got to calmer water, I noticed that Grady was still hanging on. "Wasn't that fun and exciting?" I asked him.

"Fun," Grady said, giving me a weak smile. "Exciting."

"I'm glad you guys liked that because here come the monster rapids," Tom said.

"Monster rapids? What do you mean?" Grady asked, checking his life vest straps again.

"The biggest set of rapids in the whole river," Tom said. "Heads up, guys!"

We heard the rapids before we saw them. The sound was like a train stuck in a giant blender. Tom's canoe entered the rapids first. And it headed right toward a big rock.

"Watch out!" I hollered.

It's a good thing Tom is strong. He paddled like crazy to steer the canoe to the left. He missed the rock by barely an inch.

"Tom would have been so mad if he would have smashed his new canoe," I said, shaking my head.

"Oh no, Kyle, look!" Grady said. He was pointing at the rock. We were heading right for it.

"Paddle, Grady," I yelled. I grabbed my paddle, too, but it was too late. Our raft smacked into the rock. Grady and I were both thrown into the river.

"Grab the raft!" Tom yelled.

We tried, but it was no use. The swift water was already carrying the raft down stream.

Tom turned the canoe around. He paddled to the calm, shallow water near the river's edge. "Swim to the shore," he told us.

Grady didn't need to be told twice. He started swimming and splashing toward shore like an angry shark was on his heels. But not me. I had a good grip on that big rock. No way was I was letting go.

"Kyle, you have to swim to shore," Tom shouted. "The canoe might run you over if I try to come get you."

Grady was standing in knee-deep water before he looked back and saw that I wasn't with him. I tried to put on a brave face. But Grady and I have been best friends for a long time. He must have known I was scared.

Then he did something amazing. He ran back into the river and rushed into the rapids. By the time he got to me and the rock, he was gasping for air.

"You can do it, Kyle," he said, trying to catch his breath. "We didn't take all those swimming lessons for nothing!"

Grady was right. If my best friend who was afraid of water could swim through the monster rapids, so could I. I took a deep breath. I didn't want to, but I let go of the rock.

By the time we got to shore, we were worn out. "Are you guys okay?" Tom asked as he helped us out of the cold water. "Your lips look kind of blue."

Tom had pulled his canoe up to the shore. He got some dry towels out for us. After we had warmed up a bit, I looked over at Grady and said, "I can't believe you did that for me."

Grady tried to smile. "Hey, isn't that what friends are for?"

"I'm serious," I said. "What you did was way cool."

"Kyle's right," Tom said, slapping Grady on the back. Then he added, "We had better get going, guys. Dad's going to worry when he sees your empty raft float by. There's room in the canoe for all three of us."

As we floated away from the monster rapids, I thought about what had happened. I was sure wrong about one thing. A river, a raft, and a life vest are not all you need for a good rafting trip. It also helps to have a friend.

the end.

Cookie Time

by Ella Kennen

Sadie bounded up the stairs with one thing in mind.

"Cookie time," she announced.

Cody pulled the covers over his head. "Uh-uh."

"Uh-huh," replied Sadie. "Cody, you promised."

"Yes, yes," came the muffled response from under the blankets. "At 3."

"But Cody," replied Sadie. "It is 3."

"Impossible," huffed Cody. "I just started reading."

"No, really. Check the time."

Cody poked an eye out. The big red letters on the clock read 3:00.

"Already?" complained Cody. "How did that happen?" He tossed the

blanket aside. "I guess it is cookie time."

"Yay!" Sadie said. She dragged Cody down the stairs.

As Cody listed the ingredients, Sadie dashed around the kitchen grabbing them.

"Now," Cody proclaimed, "we are ready to bake."

"Can I please pour the flour?" begged Sadie.

"Puh-lease?"

Cody bit his lip. "Okay, but be careful."

Sadie nodded. "I will."

Sadie put the measuring cup on the counter, then grabbed the bag of flour. Slowly, slowly she tipped the bag. Nothing came out. She tipped the bag a little more. Still noting. And more. Suddenly, there was flour on the counter, flour on the flour, even flour on Sadie's nose.

"Oops," she said in a tiny voice. "Sorry."

Cody sighed as he pulled out the broom. "I'm putting in the eggs."

He opened up the carton.

"Oh, no," he said.

"What's wrong?" asked Sadie.

"There's only one egg left. That's not enough."

"What are we going to do?" wailed Sadie.

Cody shrugged. "I guess we can't make cookies today."

"No! We have to make cookies today, Cody. We have to."

"Well," said Cody slowly, "we could ask Mr. Miller next door for an egg." And that's what they did.

Cody and Sadie continued cooking. They added the sugar, the butter, and the vanilla.

Suddenly, Cody smacked his forehead.

"What's wrong?" Sadie asked.

"We don't have any chocolate chips," said Cody.

"No chocolate chips!" cried Sadie. "What a disaster!"

"Well," said Cody slowly, "we could make sugar cookies instead."

"Absolutely not," replied Sadie. Her heart was set on chocolate chip today.

"What about peanut butter?" Cody suggested hopefully.

Sadie shook her head.

"I know!" she exclaimed. "I have a chocolate bar in my room I've been saving for a special occasion."

Cody chopped up the chocolate and Sadie poured the pieces into the batter. Then Sadie spooned out the cookie dough onto a baking sheet and Cody put it in the oven while Mom watched. The only thing left to do was wait.

The smell of baking cookies soon filled the air.

"Ahh," sighed Cody happily.

"Yum," agreed Sadie.

The doorbell rang.

"Who could that be?" Sadie wondered. She dashed to the door.

It was their friends from the neighborhood. "Want to build snowmen?" they asked.

"Of course!"

Sadie and Cody headed outside. They formed snowmen, snow kids, even a snow cat. Suddenly, there was an ear-splitting screech.

It took Cody a moment to figure out what was going on. "The fire alarm," he cried.

"The cookies!" he and Sadie hollered together.

Mom poked her head out. "Stay where you are."

After a bit, the alarm cut off. Then Mom came outside. "I'm sorry," she said. "The cookies burned. All your hard work for nothing."

Cody waited for a sniffle or a tear. But the perfect idea had filled Sadie's mind.

"Let's go out for apple pie!"

And that's just what they did.

the end.

The Brave Seagull

by Sara Matson

Wobble, wobble, **CRASH!** Julie's bike dumped her onto the sidewalk again. This time, she didn't get up.

"Are you hurt?" Dad asked. He handed her a tissue from his pocket.

Tears slid down Julie's cheeks. "I'll never learn to ride a bike!" she cried. "It's too hard."

"Too hard, huh?" Dad said.

Julie touched the scrape on her knee. It was oozing tiny drops of bright, red blood. "And too scary," she said. "Maybe you should put the training wheels back on."

Dad scratched his chin. "Let's take a break," he said. "We'll get you a bandage and then walk to the beach."

The beach was usually Julie's favorite place. She liked the seagulls. She liked the wet, fishy smell of the lake. She liked the shiny red popcorn wagon. But today, even though the air smelled of butter and sun sparkled like diamonds on the water, she felt grumpy. People on bicycles zoomed by. One girl tooted her horn, and Julie frowned at her.

"How about some popcorn?" Dad asked.

He bought a box of the fluffy kernels. Julie ate some, then threw a handful on the ground. Whoosh! Flapping wings filled the air. Greedy gulls gobbled up the popcorn. "More! More!" they seemed to screech like naughty children. Julie couldn't help smiling at them.

When the box was empty, the birds flew away. All except one. It was smaller than the others, and it had a scar near its eye.

"Look, Dad." Julie pointed. "What could have

happened to it?"

"Might have been a fish hook," Dad said. "Or maybe another bird attacked it."

"Poor gull," she said. "I wish I had more popcorn."

She spied a kernel under a bench. "Do you think it will take this from my hand?" she asked Dad.

"You could try," he answered.

Julie bent down and held her hand out. "Come here, gull," she said softly.

The snow-white bird stepped toward her. But when Dad moved to slap at a mosquito, it hopped away.

"It's scared," Julie said. She tried again. The gull came closer. Suddenly, Ding! The trolley car whizzed by and the gull backed away again.

"One more try," Julie whispered. "Be brave."

She held her breath. The gull hopped up to her hand. It tipped its head, like it wondered whether or not to trust her. Then, in a flash, it scooped up the popcorn and gulped it down. "More!" it cried. Julie laughed.

After watching the gull fly away, she and Dad walked home.

Dad headed for the garage. "I'll put those training wheels back on for you."

"Wait," Julie said.

Dad turned around. "What is it?"

She looked at her knee. It didn't hurt that much. "I want to try again."

It wasn't easy. She fell. She tore her jacket and skinned her elbow. But she kept on trying. And right before dinner, Julie sped down the sidewalk all by herself.

"You've got it," Dad shouted. "Keep going!"

She pedaled harder. "I'm flying!" she yelled.

Softly, she added, "Just like a seagull."

the end.

The Mysterious K.W.L.B.

by Susan Sundwall

My best buddy, Dylan, tapped me on the shoulder.

"Hey, Luke, I saw another one," he whispered

"Where?" I asked.

"Sticking out of Annie's desk. When she opened it, the card fell out." Dylan looked around the hallway, making sure nobody could hear us.

"K.W.L.B.?" I asked.

"Yeah. That's the third one this week."

The mysterious white cards with green letters were driving us nuts. Even Olivia, the smartest girl in our class, didn't know what they were. She came up behind us.

"Annie slipped the card into her backpack," said Dylan. "She walks home with Robert and Grace. We could follow them."

"Good idea!" said Olivia. "Robert and Grace have white cards too."

We agreed to follow at a distance as soon as school was out.

It made me nervous to think of following them. What if they saw us? Robert was a big kid and I didn't want to make him angry. When the last bell rang, I met Dylan and Olivia on the sidewalk.

"We can't let them know we're following them," said Dylan.

"Right," said Olivia, "talk and laugh a lot, like we don't even see them."

But we hung back too far and lost them at the

corner.

"Hey! Where'd they go?" cried Dylan.

"One of them dropped a card," I said.

Olivia bent and picked it up. "This one is different," she said.

The card had the same letters on it, but the top of each letter was curly, sort of like a tree. Olivia flipped it over. There was a map on the back.

"That's the way to Robert's house," I said. "Let's go!"

At Robert's big gray house we saw a pile of backpacks near the garage.

"Let's check the back deck," said Dylan. "You go first." He gave me a nudge.

"Oh, no. You go," I said.

"We'll all go," hissed Olivia.

As we crept near the house a strange smell drifted toward us. Something familiar. Something disgusting. What were they doing? Boiling dog food? Burping garlic? We held our noses. Olivia peeked around the corner first. She turned back with her hand over her mouth. Dylan looked next. His eyes popped wide open. I stuck out my chin, determined to look. The first thing I saw was a big sign. **K.W.L.B. Club.** Then I realized what they were doing. Each kid was eating a big bowl of cooked...broccoli!

"What are you guys doing?" Someone was behind us.

"Augh!" We all yelled at once.

It was Tom. He had a **K.W.L.B** card in his hand.

"Are you here to join the club?"

"Club?" I asked.

"The Kids Who Love Broccoli Club," he said. He grinned and held the card up.

"Robert eats broccoli?" Dylan looked stunned.

"Are you kidding," said Tom. "He's our A #1 broccoli eating champ. Today we're doing a broccoli puzzle."

Olivia slapped her forehead. "That's what **K.W.L.B.** stands for, Kids Who Love Broccoli?"

"We thought you were a secret society or something," said Dylan.

"Nah," said Tom, "we're just like you except...we like broccoli!"

"I prefer carrots," I blurted.

"Corn on the cob for me," said Dylan.

"Okay, I'll confess," said Olivia, "I love eggplant."

All three of us stared at her.

"Hey, maybe we could join the club anyway," I said. "We could change the name to K.W.L.V."

Tom looked puzzled then he said, "Oh, I get it— Kids Who Love Vegetables!"

"So what are the cards for?" asked Dylan

"Each week the club meets at a different house," said Tom. "If it's your turn, you hand out cards with a map to your house."

"Hmmm. We'd have to change the cards too," said Olivia.

"What's all the noise?" It was Robert. Something bright green stuck to his lip.

"I think we have some new members here," said Tom, "but we might need a name change."

"No problem," said Robert. "Come on back. You've gotta try the broccoli bread!"

Wow, I thought, maybe broccoli wasn't so bad after all. Dylan, Olivia and I joined them and even tried some of the bread. Then we put our heads together to figure out who would have the next meeting.

At school the next day, Olivia handed me my card.

She'd done a great job on them. I was hoping to find some other carrot lovers at lunchtime too. Mom said she'd make a carrot cake when it's my turn. Who would have thought that vegetables could be so much fun?

the end.

About Us:

Knowonder is a leading publisher of engaging, daily content that drives literacy; the most important factor in a child's success.

Parents and educators use Knowonder tools and content to promote reading, creativity, and thinking skills in children from zero to twelve.

Knowonder's Literacy Program - delivered through storybook collections - delivers original, compelling new stories every day, creating an opportunity for parents to connect to their children in ways that significantly improve their children's success.

Ultimately, Knowonder's mission is to eradicate illiteracy and improve education success through content that is affordable, accessible, and effective.

Learn more at

www.knowonder.com

Printed in Great Britain
by Amazon